More

CURIOSITIES

OF

WORCESTERSHIRE

Ann Moore

First published in Great Britain by
Eyelevel Books

ISBN 1 902528 11 5

Printed in England
by
Alden Press, Oxford

Cover and text design by Eyelevel Books, Worcester
www.eyelevelbooks.co.uk

CONTENTS

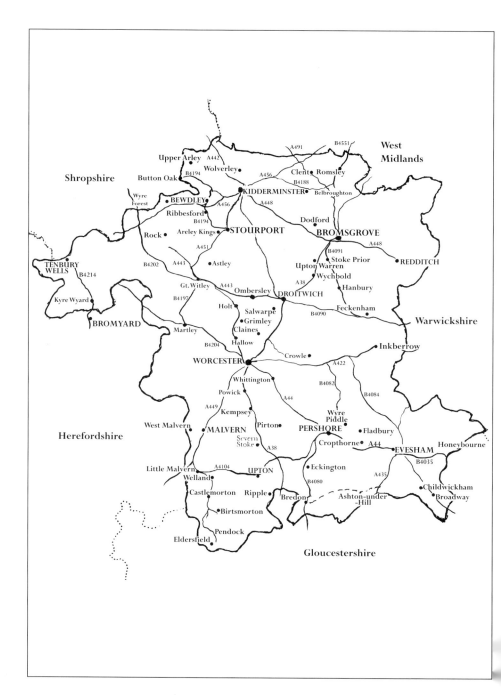

Sketch Map of Worcestershire

INTRODUCTION

In the introduction to my first book 'The Curiosities of Worcestershire' I wrote that if there was sufficient interest in the topic, we might be able to produce a second volume. Well, the interest appeared to be there and so, at last, here are more 'curiosities'. The word is used in its broadest sense and encompasses art, artefacts, buildings and memorials, most 'ancient' but a few modern – all things which I have found interesting, amusing, rare or unusual. Some were suggested by friends and acquaintances, some I have come across accidentally or through research. Some I looked for but found that they had been swept away, which is another reason for this volume – a desire to record, before they may be lost, those things which are, or could be historically significant, or which simply make one wonder or smile. I sincerely hope that those worthy of care and attention, if not already 'safe', will be preserved in some way for future generations. It would be a pity if eventually they were only remembered through my photographs.

Worcestershire is a county as diverse as any in England, with a variety of curiosities within its boundaries and some are in areas not visited in the last book. As before, they have been arranged geographically. Using Worcester as the centre, the areas radiate out towards all points of the compass. Thus it should be possible to visit more than one curiosity at the same time. Should you wish to do so, I would ask that you respect the object and wherever it may be. Some are privately owned, in which case please respect that privacy, but most may be viewed easily enough. The maps used are Ordnance Survey Landranger Maps 138, 139 and 150. The mileages are approximate and you may find an easier way of reaching your destination from your own starting point, than via the routes given here. But whether you actually visit, or are just an 'armchair investigator', I hope that you will find as much enjoyment as I have had in my collection of 'curiosities', and perhaps go on to find more of your own.

Ann Moore

WORCESTER CATHEDRAL
The Watchman's Window

Unless you look up, you are likely to miss this neat oriel window, all that is left of the Sacrist's lodging once built outside the Cathedral building and taken down in the early 1700s. It is set high into the wall of the north quire aisle, just beyond the steps to the tower. Now it faces the back of the organ which partially blocks the view, but originally it made a comfortable viewing point for the Sacrist. It was one of his duties to watch over the tombs of King John and Prince Arthur. From the Middle Ages, such tombs were jealously guarded to prevent any part of the skeleton being stolen. At that time, a bone or relic from someone revered was held in awe, since it was believed that miracles could come from touching it. In front of the High Altar, too, is buried William, the second Duke of Hamilton, who died at the Commandery on 12th September 1651 after the Battle of Worcester. The oblong brass recording his death is currently hidden beneath the carpet.

A Weighing of Souls

Facing the entrance to the Lady Chapel above the arcading to the left of the triptych.

There is so much to admire in the Cathedral that it would be easy not to notice the detail in this spandrel carving of St Peter weighing a soul. Is the figure at his feet helping or hindering? Does he wish this soul to go to heaven, or is he trying to pull him down to hell?

Whichever was intended, it shows a sculptor with a sense of humour.

And while you were admiring the work on Sir Gilbert Scott's reredos behind the High Altar, did you notice his 'signature' – 2 doves*, an emblem which he often left on his work?

They are carved in the centre of the gold work above the first double red columns on the left.

WORCESTER
A new 'Curiosity'?

High Street, opposite the Guildhall

In sharp contrast to the work of creative artists and architects of the past, here is a piece of contemporary work, work which also shows imagination and which, even now, seems to be viewed as unusual or 'curious'. These are the gates to the newly refurbished City Arcade opposite Worcester's Guildhall, (which itself has intricate 18th century cast iron gates of some importance). Our 21st century art, wrought out of galvanised steel, is the work of Herefordshire sculptor Laurence Walker. The design is made up of abstract organic shapes, but the effect is quite striking and although they have been in position for only a short time, people's reactions to them have been many and varied. A few find modern art difficult to appreciate, while others liken the abstract design to plough shares, Civil War pikes and shields, to flowers and even to squid! One

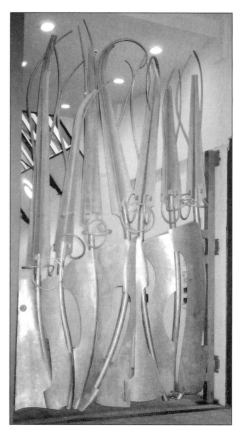

citizen declares that they represent 'a Biblical saying – it's turning spears into plough-shares ... making peace out of war'. But the sculptor, who recently graduated from the Herefordshire College of Art and Design, insists he had no particular theme in mind, and he comments that whatever point of view someone may have is a valid one. It is not certain yet whether the gates will be painted silver, but in any event, they make an interesting piece of art which may or may not be regarded as 'curious'. I like the gates, but you will have to decide for yourself.

WORCESTER

Tickets Please!

At the entrance to Crown Passage in Broad Street.

This window, tucked away as it is, must be passed, unnoticed, by hundreds of people as they cut through the passage it faces, yet over 150 years ago, many would have stopped here before they began what could be a somewhat perilous journey. It was the coming of the railways in 1850 that made this window really important. At that time passengers had to travel to Spetchley to catch a train (there was no station in Worcester), and they purchased their tickets here before clambering aboard a 'horse omnibus', 15 at a time, to rumble and sway for anything up to an hour before reaching the station. For centuries before this the Crown was a coaching inn, with a large yard, stables and commercial rooms, but although the first stagecoach was mentioned in 1674, it was some time before the first 'Flying Coach' left the Crown, on 11th June 1733, to take the hazardous journey to London, a journey which was sometimes advertised with the words 'if God permit' attached!

WORCESTER
Pause for Thought

At the Five Ways crossroads off Angel Place.

How many people in Worcester know where this studious young boy sits? Pausing from his writing, he looks heavenward, perhaps in the sculptor's mind, seeking inspiration – although now the fanciful might imagine that he is asking that the constant noise below him might cease, so that he could concentrate! This pupil sits above the still impressive Congregational Church at a crossing where cars pass ceaselessly. He symbolises the aspirations of the Rev. George Osborn who, in 1797, began the first school here for the poor. It started as a Sunday School, first for boys, then for girls, teaching children not only the Bible, but also how to read, write and spell. Good attendance and behaviour were rewarded with gifts of clothing. The present building, designed by the noted architect Sir Aston Webb, was begun in 1888, encompassing 22 classrooms and a hall at a cost of £7,000. The classrooms, on ground and first floors, surround the main hall with its small raised platform (for the teachers in assembly!), and they still have their long glass interior windows, so popular with the builders of Victorian schools.

WORCESTER
Home of the B.M.A.

Off Infirmary Walk, near Pitchcroft, at the foot of Castle Street.

Most patients visiting Worcester's Infirmary go in through another door and are not expected to enter via these imposing steps which lead into a once important Georgian hospital. Begun in 1768 to a design by Anthony Keck, the Royal Infirmary succeeded Worcester's first hospital (1746) in Silver Street – at that time only the seventh public hospital of its kind in England, but fast becoming too small. This new Infirmary cost £6000, a brickworks was set up on Pitchcroft to help supply the builders and it was declared open in 1771, here on the corner of Salt Lane, (Castle Street from 1813). Many of its wards were named after benefactors of the Silver Street site – Bishop Maddox, Sir John Rushout, and Edward Garlick of Bristol who bought the land in Salt Lane for this new hospital. The most memorable person connected with the Infirmary must be Sir Charles Hastings, a Rector's son from Martley, born 1794, who became a great medical pioneer and who, in this building's Board Room in July 1832, called a meeting which eventually led to the founding of the British Medical Association. Knighted in 1850, Sir Charles lived for some time in a gracious house, 43 Foregate Street, and on his death, aged 72, he was buried in Astwood Cemetary.

WORCESTER
Welcome to the Gardens

To the east of the city, behind the library, on the corner of Sansome Walk and Arboretum Rd.

The names Sansome Walk and Arboretum indicate that at one time this area was 'country' favoured by Worcester citizens for 'promenading'. In the mid 1850s, in an effort to maintain it as such, the land was bought by the Worcester Pleasure Grounds Co. Ltd. Here they designed formal walks and terraces, flower beds and a fountain, greens for archery and bowls, a cricket ground and a splendid glass pavilion. Arboretum Lodge stood at the entrance to the Gardens, flanked by wrought iron gates (now standing at the entrance to the hospital in Infirmary Walk). The Pleasure Gardens opened on 30th July 1859 to great acclaim. But all this had cost a great deal of money and in spite of fetes and shows and many attractions, the Company went into liquidation four years later and the land was sold. By now railways had arrived, there was a need for housing, and planners gave little thought to the environment. The fine pleasure gardens were lost to the city and green was covered by concrete. Now all that remains to remind us of what might have been, is the pattern of streets where garden avenues were, and this striking building which now houses offices for small modern businesses.

WORCESTER

An Ancient Granary

In the Lyppards area of the Warndon Estate, at the end of Trotshill Lane East.
Map reference: O.S. map 150 (1:50,000); 887558.

This small but once much used granary stands almost forgotten now, its back to a modern motor-way, and although it is listed, few know it is here. Built in the late 17th century – part of the flooring re-uses wood with the date 1660 inscribed – it is interesting in being set on stad-dle stones. There are three rows of three stones which

were more often used beneath hay ricks to prevent vermin, and here they keep the building off the ground. Any vermin still getting in could be caught by the cat – and if you thought a cat door is a modern invention, then you would be wrong. Records show that, hidden by the modern protective door, and beside the original 17th century one, with its decorative strap hinges, is a small circular door for the cats. Sadly,

the owner was not able to let me photograph this unique feature, which must surely be of interest to anyone appreciative of curiosities! The Granary is privately owned and easily seen from the roadside and because of its con-dition should only be viewed in this way.

CLAINES
Prayers and Pints

½ mile north of Worcester City boundary off A449.
Map Reference; O.S. map 150 (1:50,000); 842588

The Mug House at Claines is a unique hostelry, for it is said to be the only public house in England in a churchyard. When it was built at least 600 years ago, this was quite commonplace, for the land often belonged to the Church and agreements were reached whereby a landlord could hold the licence if the Church received a percentage of his profits. Gatherings at a church ale-house were popular, especially during a long service –

> '*About Mid-service, they goe in a Rowe*
> *After the Priest, into the Church-ale-house*
> *(Which in the churchyard standeth) ...* **

– and a Claines parish document records that as early as 1538, Vestry meetings were held there. It also notes that in 1784 the ale bill for such a meeting was £3. 15d – at a time when a new cloth for the Communion table cost 2s 11d! The name 'Mug House' was common when gentlemen reached an agreement over a mug of ale, although it is suggested that here the name may be connected with the old Communion plate. Indeed, a Bishop's crozier was found buried in the building when work was undertaken some time ago. Happily the connection with the church here is still strong – lack of space elsewhere has necessitated a room in the Mug House being used for some Sunday School lessons.

* *Verse part of an unpublished poem by Jervis Markham, gent, 1600, referring to a visit he made to St James Church in Colwall, near Malvern.*

DROITWICH
Magnificent Mosaics

Left of B4090 from Worcester, ¼ mile beyond the Celvestune Way roundabout on the outskirts of Droitwich.
Map Reference: O.S. map 150 (1: 50,000); 895621.

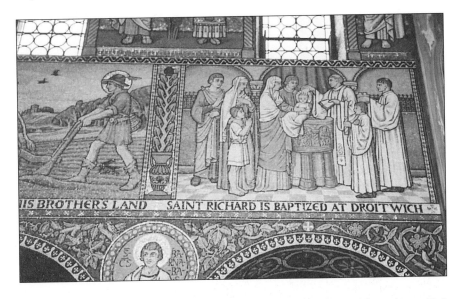

Enter the Roman Catholic Church of the Sacred Heart and these beautiful mosaics will take your breath away. They glow on the walls, ceiling and in the side chapel, each picture telling a story in the life of Droitwich's own patron saint St Richard, who was born in 1197. Reputed to be the finest mosaics outside Westminster Cathedral, they were the dedicated work of sculptor and interior designer Gabriel Pippet who, with the help of two other craftsmen, spent eleven years of his life creating this Byzantine style interior in a church which was only built in 1921. Inspired by having seen such work in Ravenna in Italy, Pippet created his masterpieces using thousands of tiny squares of brightly coloured Venetian glass which were painstakingly set into layers of mastic. The work was completed in 1932 and forms a magnificent memorial to its creator, who died thirty years later, as well as to St Richard of Droitwich who rose to become Bishop of Chichester. A statue to him stands in Vine's Park near the site of a great salt pit which, after failure, is said to have flourished when he blessed it. There is much of interest in Droitwich, and the good TIC in Victoria Square can provide informative leaflets. It is open Mon-Sat from 10am to 4pm.

DROITWICH
A Pilgrim Father

1 mile from Droitwich centre, up the Holloway off B4090.
Map Reference: O.S. map 150 (1: 50,000): 903625.

This plaque to Edward Winslow, one of Worcestershire's early, more adventurous sons, is on the north wall of the nave in the church of St Peter de Witton, where Edward was baptised on 20th October 1595. The first of eight children of a prosperous yeoman, also Edward, of Kempsey, he was educated at King's School, Worcester, before becoming a printer in London. He travelled to Holland in 1617, but returned to Southampton to join other pilgrims aboard the Mayflower, as they prepared to seek the New World. With 100 passengers and a crew of 40, the Mayflower set sail in September 1620, but it was 66 days before they eventually landed in America and founded a colony at New Plymouth, now Massachusetts. In the years that followed, Edward was elected Governor three times. It is thought that yellow fever brought about his death as he voyaged between Hispaniola and Jamaica in his later role as a civil commissioner, and he was buried at sea with a 20 gun salute on 8th May, 1655. St Peter's church itself is well maintained and has some Norman work, but is mainly 12th and 14th century.

DROITWICH
A Dolls' House

In the One Stop Council Shop at the junction of the B 4090 and the High Street.

These dolls have thwarted any attempt to move them from their home, a home they have lived in for hundreds of years. They are copies of 16th century jack-in-a-box dolls, but no-one knows just how old they are. They were found in the eaves of the 15th century building long known as Bullock's Cafe, in 1996 when it was being renovated to become the Council Shop. Their initial removal coincided with a heavy storm and water pouring through the building, with electric cables being accidentally cut and illness, and some called them 'devil dolls' – those dolls sometimes used to curse an enemy in the superstitious 16th century. But I prefer to think that they were, in fact, precious toys, placed in the wall for safety or to bring good luck. In any event, about ten inches tall, with painted faces and muslin cloaks, they sit now in their glass case in the reception area, surveying the world benignly enough, safe in the knowledge that no-one is going to risk moving them again.

HANBURY
A Travel Victim

12 miles north east of Worcester, on a minor road off B4090.
Map Reference: O.S. map 150 (1: 50,000); 954644.

It is worth visiting Hanbury's 12th century church if only to sit and enjoy the magnificent panoramic views over South Worcestershire. St Mary's stands in a peaceful and elevated position on what was once an Iron Age hill fort. Its nave and aisles medieval, it is an impressive building, used regularly, although otherwise often locked. This unusual pictorial epitaph to Henry Parry, however, can be found among graves to the right of the church. Henry, it would appear, died as the result of an accident on 2nd July 1847 when in the 21st year of his life. The suddeness of his demise led George and Sarah, his grieving parents, to warn that

Our life hangs by a single thread
It/To? soon is cut and we are dead ...

The inscription will soon be as difficult to read, as is that to Richard Hussey, Clerk of Hanbury Parish and 'Father of the Musical Society'. His epitaph is unusual in having as part of it, the music stave and the first four bars of Handel's 'Messiah' –

'I know that my Redeemer liveth ...'

Sadly this stone, beyond Harry's and further to the right, leans ever nearer the ground as the months go by.

FECKENHAM
The Man who Died Twice?

6 miles from Droitwich along the B4090 to Alcester, off High Street.
Map Reference: O.S. map 150 (1: 50,000); 001616

This curious gravestone lies to the right of the path in Feckenham's neat church grounds.

> *'Here Lieth the body of John Collier he died on the six & twentieth day of June an dom 1671 Being aged 40' (sic)*

Does this mean Mr Collier appeared dead on the 6th, but revived to finally die on the 20th?

If so, one can understand why his family recorded this on a headstone. Or is this a rather unusual way of noting the 26th of June? If it is, the stonemason gave himself more work while making us wonder! The top of the stone is graced by a rather crudely incised skull with cross-bones either side, and thanks to a local gentleman, met by chance, and a soft brush he then brought from home, we were able to decipher the rest of the poorly executed and worn lettering. The verse (often used) reads:

> *Behold all you that passeth by*
> *As you are now so once was I*
> *As I am now so you must (be)*
> *When this you (see) then think (of me)*
> *And sure the Lord your lives amend*
> *And think upon your latter end.*

Some things never change over the centuries.

WYCHBOLD
An unsolved Mystery

North of Droitwich, 1 mile beyond motorway junction on A38, turning off on to a minor road, signposted Stoke Works.
Map Reference: O.S. map 150 (1: 50,000) 930659.

In the north west of the churchyard of St Mary's church lies yet another unusual gravestone, one which no-one seems able to explain. I have researched among church registers, local documents and old parish magazines, but as yet have found no reference as to why it should be here, bottle shaped as it is, *'In memory of fifty infants gathered into their Saviour's bosom'*. It is undated and bears no name. It cannot have a long history, for the church was only completed in 1888, both money and land for it and the vicarage being provided by John Corbett of the Chateau Impney. The most likely explanation is that it was here in this churchyard in the 1890s, that children from the surrounding area, who had died from cholera, were buried. At that time, it was generally considered better for all victims to be buried in one place. It is strange, though, that there is, as far as I can see, no reference to this being the case. And who donated this gravestone as a memorial, and when – and why in this shape? I should be very happy to hear from anyone who can shed light on the mystery.

UPTON WARREN
A Numerical Puzzle.

5 miles from Droitwich, just beyond Webb's Garden Centre and west of A38.
Map Reference: O.S. map 150 (1: 50,000); 930675.

The Reverend Hooper, for 52 years Rector of the Church of St Michael until his death aged 78 in 1888, was a numerologist and a great exponent of symbolism. His marble cross, atop 3 granite steps, is situated beside the south wall of the church. Facing the path are carved the Christian symbol of a fish and the Latin *'carpe diem'*, (enjoy the moment). The crostic, however, which puzzles everyone, is at the back of the cross. I am indebted to Mike Wall for passing on an article by Vivian Bird which provides an explanation. Apparently the Rev. Hooper, in an obscure book, explained that the middle letter of the Greek word for fish, *'has the numerical value of 9, or the square of 3, the number of the Trinity, thus stamping the superlative of the Trinity on the central point of the Cross ... 18 is the number of the Beast'*. He went on to say that since 6 additions on the pedestal (3 down, 2 diagonal and the 3 sixes across) add up to 18, he believed that *'the Cross, or the Kingdom of Christ, tramples on the darker pedestal of his adversary the Devil'*. With logic such as this and the fanaticism to design his own headstone, one wonders if his parishioners found the Rev. Hooper's sermons as obscure as all this might suggest!

STOKE PRIOR
Tribute to a 'Salt King'

2 miles north east of Wychbold on B4091.
Map Reference: O.S. map 150 (1: 50,000); 949677

This fine east window in the chancel at St Michael's is a tribute to Droitwich's 'salt king' John Corbett, who was responsible for financing the church's restoration programme in 1894/5. St Michael's dates back to the 12th century, the tower to the 13th, and there was probably a church here in Saxon times. The restoration of this Norman building, when the only roof not replaced was the 15th century one in the south aisle, cost John Corbett at least £4,500 – at that time a sum equivalent to 265 years average pay of a salt miner. But the window pays tribute not only to Corbett's generosity, but also to his philanthropy, to the fact that in 1859 he had abolished female labour in his salt works. He was a pioneer in this, for the Factory Act of 1850 only applied to textile factories and merely shortened the working hours of women and children. Corbett raised his men's wages to make up for the loss of women's pay, provided housing and built a school. John Corbett may have been a shrewd and exacting business man, but he appears to have shown consideration toward his workers at a time when social reform was in its infancy.

STOKE PRIOR
Above Worldly Ways

To the left of Corbett's memorial window and high above the organ, one can see this lancet window – without glass and looking out of a small room once said to have been the cell of a religious recluse, an Anchorite. The room, above the sacristy, was examined and then closed off at the time of the church restoration. At that time it was recorded that 'some human bones and fragments of carved alabaster were found beneath its floor' and a small section of Norman fresco painting, the colours still bright and thought to be decoration of a semicircular window head, was also uncovered on the south wall. During the 14th and 15th centuries Anchorites (from the Greek 'anchores', meaning 'I withdraw') withdrew from the world to live in prayer. Were this the case here, the holy man would never leave the room, seeing the villagers of Stoke Prior only through his window, relying on them to provide food, and in return listening to confidences, praying with them or offering counsel if requested.

BROMSGROVE
Visit from an 'Honest Man'

On the A38 from Wychbold, near the junction of B4091 and A448.
Map Reference: O.S. map 139 (1: 50,000); 957705.

The Black Cross, built in the mid 1600s at this crossroads where once a gibbet stood, is now Bromsgrove's oldest inn, the only one which was trading at the time of the Civil War. Around that time, in 1651, Bromsgrove was *'merely a scattering village'*, but the Black Cross had beside it a sandstone smithy (to the right of the picture and now white-washed). It was here, after his mare had cast a shoe, that Charles II stopped on his way to the coast after his defeat at the Battle of Worcester. Dressed quietly in grey, like a farmer's son in his best attire and apparently 'servant' to Mrs Jane Lane who rode behind him, 'Will Jackson' stood talking to the smith as he worked, agreeing with the man that 'that rogue Charles Stewart ... deserved to be hanged' for the trouble he'd caused. 'Upon which', the King said later to diarist Samuel Pepys, 'he said that I spoke like an honest man, and so we parted.'

Later, in the 1840s, the Black Cross became a coaching inn, and at that time 59 inns or beerhouses were listed in Bromsgrove – a ratio of one public house to every 160 people; but then, of course, Bromsgrove was home to the nailing industry and the inns also catered for thirsty nailers. A great many have since been demolished, but the Black Cross, extended now, survives along with its ghosts, and appears to flourish.

DODFORD

A Reformer's Village

3 miles north west of Bromsgrove, off A448.
Map Reference: O.S. map 139 (1: 50,000); 933724.

Dodford church stands above the village scattered at its feet. Built in 1907/8, it is unusual in having a timbered cloister and an outside pulpit on the tower wall facing the courtyard. It also houses the best collection of early 20th century Arts and Crafts work in the country, created by the Bromsgrove Guild – but the village came into being before this church did.

Dodford is unique in being one of four villages laid out by social reformers, although in the 12th century there was a Priory here. The reformers, Chartists, aimed to better the lives of industrial workers by giving them the opportunity of buying land and a home in the country. To this end, Feargus O'Connor (1794-1855), M.P. and leader of the Movement, formed the National Land Company, buying land here in Dodford where he built 43 houses, most with an allotment of 3 or 4 acres. The houses were distinctive, the forerunner of the modern bungalow, with a wide central gable over the front door. But their occupants, mostly nailers from Bromsgrove, had no agricultural background and the soil was heavy and difficult to work and disillusioned, they soon drifted back to the work they knew. Soon the houses were sold off, and now they have been modernised and many hide behind high hedges. Ironically, many are occupied by commuters who work out of the village in towns nearby. Perhaps O'Connor would not be surprised.

(The church is generally open on Tuesdays, though a key may be obtained nearby if it is not.)

BELBROUGHTON
The Cutting Edge

4 miles north of Dodford, south of A491 on B4188.
Map Reference: O.S. map 139 (1: 50,000): 920768.

If you enter this delightful village from Dodford, its peaceful air belies an unexpected industrial heritage. In the 18th and 19th centuries it rang to the sound of machinery and hammer on metal. Belbroughton was home to iron forges. Indeed, records of such work go back to the mid 16th century, but the most important forges were those in the late 1800s, owned by Isaac Nash who made his name famous all over the world through his manufacture of sythes, hooks and hay knives. The industry is commemorated by this steam hammer preserved on the village green by the local History Society and the Parish Council. It was made by Bradley and Sons in the U.S.A. in 1897, and was used in one of Nash's Sythe Works until 1968 when the last one closed. He began his work in 1835 with 2 employees, but by 1881 he had a workforce of 105 men and 5 boys. Now this industry here is only a memory, although at least one of his buildings still stands, down by the mill stream at the foot of Forge Alley nearby. Small trading industries work in that area now.

BELBROUGHTON
'Talbott, our Goode Dogge'

To the left of the village green.

Belbroughton is not alone in having a hostelry called The Talbot. But why is there a picture of a dog? (and a dog which here actually says 'woof woof'!). The first written link of dog and name is seen in a poem written by Chaucer in 1449, but there it was the dog's name – *'That is Talbott, our goode dogge'*. Later, in 1562, the dog is referred to as a breed thought to have been brought to England by a member of the Talbot family. It was a variety of hound, generally light coloured, with a great sense of smell and therefore known to have great tracking abilities. At that time a writer called Leigh wrote about *'A Talbot with coller ... ... these houndes pursue the foote of pray, by scente of ye same orels by ye bloud thereof'* (sic). The Talbot was especially used for stag hunting in the 1800s – and since hunting is generally associated with a celebratory drink, perhaps that's why pubs have taken the name.

ROMSLEY
Is it a Folly?

On Romsley Hill, 8 miles north of Bromsgrove on minor road between A491 and B4451.
Map Reference: O.S. map 139 (1: 50,000); 958785

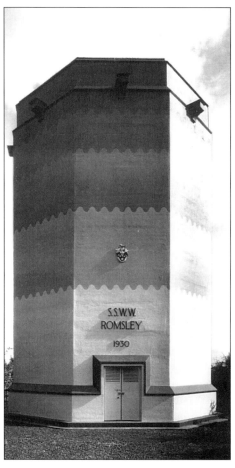

Leaving Fairfield and crossing the A491 to approach Romsley, you could be forgiven for thinking that the north of the county has its own Folly. In the distance, high on the hill, you occasionally see between the trees, a tall tower, rather like a castle and painted a striking shade of blue. Closer inspection, however, reveals it to be, not a Folly, but a service reservoir owned and maintained by the South Staffordshire Water Company. Standing 15 or 16 metres high and built of reinforced concrete, it came into service in 1931, and since then has been supplying the Romsley area with fresh water taken from the Churchill and Hagley pumping stations. The water level is monitored by telemetry at Walsall. Whoever thought of painting the tower shades of blue graduating to white at the base, should be congratulated, for, although arresting, it is more interesting than it would have been, had it been left as mere grey concrete.

CROWLE

Tithes Please.

7 miles northeast of Worcester off A 538. Down Bredicott Lane, beyond the church.
Map Reference: O.S. map 150 (1: 50,000); 922558.

This sadly delapidated 14th century tithe barn is about to disappear, but hopefully, since it is listed, parts of it at least will be rebuilt to something like its former self. Probably built by the Priors of Worcester as part of the manor of Crowle, it originally extended to the roadside and had 7 bays, and we have a record of someone who would have known it well when it was in its prime. Prior More *'took the tonsure'* in 1488 when he was 16 and became Prior of Worcester from 1518 to 1536. Then he resigned and after leaving the Monastery had use of the manor house at Crowle and at Grimley, his parents' home. His resignation was forced upon him when one of his Monks, John Musard, charged him with having too lavish a life style – a charge which proved well founded when an inventory was made at Crowle on his death in 1588. His chambers were *'hanged with peynted clothes'*, he had *'fether beddes'* and many *'blanckettes'* and *'coverlettes'*, and *'a pyllow of downe of an ell (45 ins) long'*. His cope was *'of blewe felvet with Oysters fethers'* and he had a *'newe myter with many peerls and other precius stones &c'*. Bearing in mind that he also had *'cxx peyer of pigions'*, it is more than likely that this tithe barn was full to overflowing with riches too! One could wish to have visited it when Prior More was there. How different it would have looked then.

WHITTINGTON
A Barrow Of Mystery

½ mile south east of Worcester, off A44 just before M5 junction.
Map Reference: O.S. map 150 (1: 50,000); 874523

Much has been written about Crookbarrow Hill, or the Whittington Tump as it is known locally, simply because it is there. No-one is sure of its history. It is an accepted feature of the landscape, but still something of a curiosity, an 'elliptical mound' rising to a vertical height of 50 feet, known and used since prehistoric times and probably worked by man to give it its present shape. A Neolithic scraper has been found there, as have Roman coins, and the buried remains of a motte castle are known to be on the summit (a garrison fort of the type introduced by the Normans). Was this mound artificially enlarged to its present 350m x 250m size for religious reasons, or because of its strategic position? Its name comes from the Old English '*Cruc*' meaning 'barrow or tumulous', and '*Beorg*', also meaning 'barrow'. Yet it isn't a burial ground, so the name must refer to its shape rather than to its function. Now a scheduled ancient monument, Crookbarrow Hill holds on to its secrets, and until they are fully revealed, it will retain that air of mystery which sets people wondering.

PERSHORE
A Monks' Bridge

9 miles south of Worcester along A44.
Map Reference: O.S. map 150 (1:50,000); 952451

This is the only remaining monastic bridge in Worcestershire and it has had an eventful history. From early days this was an important river crossing point on the route between London and Aberystwyth. It is possible that the river was originally bridged here as early as the 7th century, but the first documentary evidence we have is in 1290 when one Nicholas du Muthon left 12d 'for repair of Pershore Bridge'. We know that there had long been a Benedictine Monastery in Pershore, but it was in 1413 that the Monks officially reconstructed the bridge after an Abbot and his retinue were drowned when his boat capsized. During the Civil War, in June 1644, Charles I ordered the centre of it to be blown up in the face of the Parliamentarians, and the order was carried out so promptly that 40 Royalists were drowned Repairs were later made using stones from the ruins of Elmley Castle. The bridge was still in regular use until the new one was opened in 1926, made of concrete and the first in Worcestershire to be specifically so built to take 'modern' traffic. Still the Avon flows peacefully beneath this medieval bridge, a river which grew as an important waterway for freight such as wool, grain and building materials, only to fade with the coming of the railways.

PERSHORE
'Dragon's Teeth'

Beside the Monks' Bridge by the A44.

These strange concrete objects, cylindrical and 2ft across, are all that is left of mobile tank barriers designed for use on metalled roads, which were brought here in July 1940. As part of the war defences, they were to be hauled into position (hence the hole in the top for a crowbar), across the main road at the bridge and set in staggered lines, with bricks scattered among them. Only these 4 are left, securely anchored as a barrier to vehicles at the end of the old bridge. Weir Meadow was part of an inland defence line from the Welsh borders to the Wash – the 'GHQ Stop Line' – to prevent the enemy advancing through England, later a very real threat as the war advanced and Hitler stood just across the Channel. This inland defence involved the tank barriers and mines, 7 foot metal rails set in concrete, steel hawsers set across the river and 2 gun emplacements, or 'pill boxes', which housed mortar firing artillery and guns, at first manned round the clock by 5 men. All that remains of those now, are the foundations in the car park. Not far from here, at Wick, there was also a radar-control room which was still in operation at the beginning of the 1950s. Our country at war was nothing if not prepared, but how much our defences have had to advance over the decades.

PERSHORE
A Thing of Beauty …

In Pershore Abbey.

This beautiful sculpture which graces Pershore Abbey above the altar is not old, as such work usually is, but modern in more ways than one. It is the work of Linda Mance who now lives in retirement in Cropthorne, and it is but one of many such pieces she has created, including figures which illustrate the story of John Bunyan's 'Pilgrim's Progress'. Mrs Mance won a scholarship to Art School in 1929 when she was 13, but it was not until 1979 that she began this type of creative work. Then she took a 5 day course at the Women's Institute Denman College – a course in paper sculpture. This remarkable sculpture in the Abbey, inspired by the figure of Christ which overlooks Rio in Brazil, is indeed made of paper, an incredible work of art which so resembles stone. Many will hope that it will survive to stay in the Abbey for a long time to come, for not only is it a thing of beauty in itself, but its being above the altar provides a comforting image and is said to be most helpful in worship.

ECKINGTON

'These Eloquent Grooves'

5 miles south of Pershore on B4080.
Map Reference: O.S. map 150 (1,50,000); 922424

Here we meet another old bridge, said to be the oldest over the Avon, and documents record that in 1440 it had 7 arches and was of timber. In the mid 1630s, when it was made navigable between Tewkesbury and Warwick, the Avon became the first river in the country to have lock gates. So, in 1685, Eckington bridge was given stone piers, upon which in 1729, new arches were built of Ombersley stone. By now the river could accomodate ships of up to 30 tons – great flat-bottomed barges full of coal, grain, sugar and iron, helped along by large square sails – until they came to the bridge. Then man power came into play, for there was no tow-path for horses. The bow hauliers stood on the bridge and pulled the boat as close as possible to the centre arch. Holding fast, the spare end of the rope was then dropped over the parapet on the upstream side, from where it floated back down under the bridge to the boat and was made fast. This end then took the strain, while the other end was detached. Thus were made the grooves noted by

Quiller Couch in his poem about Eckington Bridge* in 1896. In the 19th century the Wharf, known as The Nap and now a picnic site, was a place where Eckington farmers came down to water their cattle.

*   *...But yet these eloquent grooves remain,*
        Worn in the sandstone parapet hour by hour
        By labouring bargemen where they shifted ropes ...

ECKINGTON
Here Lies an Artist

1 mile south of Eckington Bridge on B4080
Map Reference: O.S.map 150 (1: 50,000) ; 922414

Modern headstones rarely illustrate the life of the deceased. That type of memorial had its heyday in Victorian times, and they do make churchyard detective work more interesting. Here is an example still legible in spite of some weathering. As you can see, Mr Henry Kay was an artist, there can be no doubt about that. He was born in Birmingham in 1824, but spent 30 years in Eckington and died on 11th July 1901. In 1860 his work was recognised as having some merit, for we are told that in that year he became a 'National Medallist'. He pre-deceased his wife Elizabeth by nearly 17 years and she lies here with him. His family was obviously very proud of his talents.

BREDON
Here Lies my Heart

17 miles south of Worcester, 3 miles northeast of Tewkesbury, just north of B4080
Map Reference: O.S. map 150 (1: 50,000): 920370

The tall and graceful spire draws you to Bredon's Norman Church of St Giles and once there, there is much to see, not least the splendidly ornate Jacobean memorial to Sir Giles Reed, *'a worthy Squire ... hardie, and wise, and just ...'* who died in 1611. But nearby lies the tomb of an 'unknown warrior', a Crusader. Beneath his shield, his hands hold his heart, sent home from the Holy Land where this knight died, probably about 1290. It was often a Knight's wish that, should he die when far from home, his heart should be returned to his family or place of birth for burial. Such memorials, when one finds them, which is not often, are generally smaller (the one at Castle Frome in Herefordshire is only a few inches high) One cannot help but wonder who this man was, what he was like and if his family felt that his sacrifice was a worthy one.

BREDON
A Door on High

as opposite; 17 miles south of Worcester, 3 miles northeast of Tewkesbury, just north of B4080
Map Reference: O.S. map 150 (1: 50,000): 920370

Still on the south side of the church is the low outline of a window, once probably there as a Confessional, an open air Confessional. Before being blocked it would have had an iron grill and a small wooden door.

Turning to retrace your steps to leave the church, you may be startled to see a narrrow door set high in the wall above the porch without any means of entry. This unusual feature was a parvis, a small room which was possibly used by Monks to store documents or valuables, or which served as a room for a visiting priest. It would have been reached by a ladder from the floor of the nave.

Outside and across from the church, notice the small figures of Charles II and Oliver Cromwell on the Rectory roof (if they move, the end of the world is nigh!) and one of the largest tithe barns in England, now in the care of the National Trust.

ASHTON UNDER HILL
For the Penitent

7 miles south of Evesham off A 435, on the lower slopes of Bredon hill
Map Reference: O.S. map 150 (1:50,000); 997377.

As you approach the lych gate of this parish church, you are met by a fine example of a Weeping Cross, 15th century and almost complete except for the very top which has been replaced by a sundial. Since it is so near the church, it is unlikely to have been used as a preaching cross. Instead, wrong-doers would be forced to confess their sins and kneel to do penance here. The stocks which would be nearby are no longer there. The church itself was probably Norman on Saxon foundations, but little of that remains. Much of it is 14th to 17th century, altered in the 19th century, and an informative leaflet inside the church will tell you something of its history. One interesting floor memorial is that to Frances, daughter of John Baldwin who died on 3rd April 1750, aged 13 years, 8 months and 7 days – obviously a much lamented child.

ASHTON UNDER HILL
Where Lightning Strikes

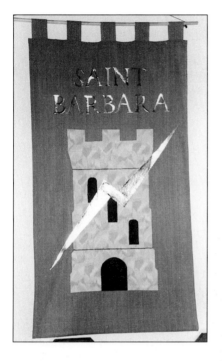

This is the only church in England, apart from one in the Coventry Diocese, to be dedicated to the Virgin Martyr, St Barbara, but this dedication only took place in 1750. Prior to that, the church was known as St Andrews, but St Martin and St Barbara were the patron saints of the monks of St Barb-en-Ange in Normandy who owned the manor of Beckford in the Middle Ages. St Barbara is something of an enigma, indeed no-one is sure if she really existed, but legend has it that she lived in the 3rd or 4th century, the daughter of a pagan. When she converted to Christianity, her angry father locked her in a tower, arranging to have 2 windows cut into it for light. In his absence she persuaded the workmen to cut 3, in honour of the Holy Trinity. On finding 3 windows, her father, beside himself with rage, killed her with his sword, but as he did so, lightning struck the weapon and he too was killed. Thus one of her emblems is the zig zag flash of lightning. Because of the violent nature of her death, she in invoked against thunder and lightning and accidents resulting from explosions. She is the patron saint of armourers and gunsmiths and the Royal Artillery wear her zig zag flash. Her other emblem is, as you see, a tower with 3 windows, making her also the patron saint of builders. Her Saint's Day is 4th December.

FLADBURY
A Tale of Two Mills

6 miles northeast of Pershore, between A44 and B4084 Worcester to Evesham roads.
Map Reference: O.S. map 150 (1:50,000): 998462

Fladbury has boasted two working mills from at least 1302, when they were valued at £3.19.6d. They appear either side of you when you stand on a grassy area, once called 'the coal wharf', beside the river. Both mills changed and expanded over the centuries. They ground corn, made cider from local apples, and in 1635 the owner of Fladbury Mill, William Sandys, invested money to make the Avon navigable from Stratford to Tewkesbury. Now coal could be delivered (hence 'the wharf') and other goods moved away. In 1899 Fladbury Mill was instrumental in supplying electricity for street lighting and for some private houses, one of the first villages to have this – 'a penny per night, per light, perhaps' the saying went!

Somewhat confusingly, this mill on the weir is called Cropthorne Mill, although the pretty village which bears its name is about a mile away. This is because the parish boundary between Fladbury and Cropthorne runs mid-river below the mills, then joins the left bank, so that the greater part of the weir is in Fladbury, leaving this mill in Cropthorne. 'Cropthorne' ceased being a working mill well before 'Fladbury' did and hasn't worked as such for more than 100 years. Refurbished, it now stands proudly by the weir, like 'Fladbury' a private home, much photographed but naturally not open to visitors, and reached by a private ferry operated by a chain.

WYRE PIDDLE
A Watery Diamond

On the River Avon, 1 mile north of Pershore
Map Reference: O.S. map 150 (1: 50,000): 959469

Ask anyone to describe the shape of a lock on canal or river and they might say 'oblong?,' 'lozenge shaped?' But here is one which does not conform to this general rule. Wyre Lock is diamond shaped and always

has been. This is because the soil is so light that a lock of the usual design wouldn't exist for long – it would cave in. However, building it to this rough diamond pattern means that its very shape acts as an arch, spreading the weight load so that the soil all round the sides remains in place. Wyre Lock was completely restored and re-opened in September 1954, with new lock gates and approaches, and then refurbished in the winter of 1994/95. But each time its historical shape was retained, making it an unusual if watery curiosity for inclusion here. Chadbury Lock had been diamond shaped, too, until it was rebuilt with parallel sides in 1953. It is difficult to reach Wyre Lock on foot, but anyone navigating the Lower Avon will certainly be familiar with it.

EVESHAM
Measure the Miles

Abbey Gate, Merstow Green, 16 miles south east of Worcester along A44 or B4084
Map Reference: O.S. map 150 (1: 50,000);

This old milestone has seen many changes in transport during its lifetime, and originally it stood at the crossroads at the top of Greenhill. The first to consult it were perhaps travellers on foot or on horse-back, then coaches and carriages passed it by, before cars finally stirred up the dust around it. Dating from 1730, it reads

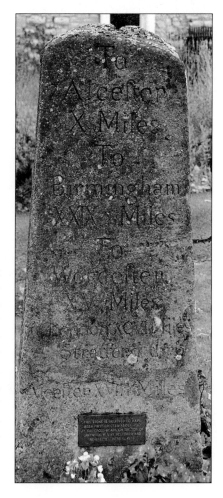

To Alcester

X miles

To Birmingham

XXIX miles

To Worcester

XV miles

London XCVI miles

Stratford thru

Alcester XVIII miles

Since 1978 it has stood safely among the flowers in the garden of the Almonry, the building once home to the Monk from the Benedictine Abbey who was responsible for the welfare of the poor and sick in the town. The building dates from at least 1400 and is Grade 1 star listed. Here you will now find the museum and its unique display of Evesham's history, as well as all the information you could wish in the busy and efficient TIC.

EVESHAM
In Memory of an Earl

1 mile north of Evesham centre, along the Squires, near the junction of A4538 and B4184.
Map Reference: O.S. map 150 (1: 50,000): 030458.

Standing high on Greenhill in fields which once ran red with blood, Leicester Tower commemorates the life of an Earl who died in battle nearly 600 years before the memorial itself was built. The Battle of Evesham took place here on 4th August 1265 when Simon de Montford, leading the barons against his brother in law Henry III 'fought stoutly like a giant for the liberties of England'. The fighting was fierce, 4,000 soldiers were killed and, defeated at last, Simon de Montford was captured, hung, drawn and quartered and finally buried in Evesham's Abbey Church. But the principles of democracy had been set, for de Montford had earlier, by the Provisions of Oxford in 1258, imposed reforms which gave the barons a say in Parliament. The clash when the King tried to restore power eventually led to the battle. Perhaps that is why, in 1845, Edward Rudge built this handsome tower to reflect the importance of Simon de Montford, Earl of Leicester. The battle itself is commemorated by an Obelisk which can be reached by a walkway and over several stiles beyond the Tower. At the end of the 1990s the area was redeveloped to include dwellings, but a board by the battlefield site shows the lines of public access in Abbey Manor Park.

EVESHAM
Open Wide

In the riverside Walkman Gardens, beside the A44 opposite the Northwick Hotel.
Map Reference: O.S. Map 150: (1: 50,000): 040435.

Walk along the Waterside towards the town centre and eventually you will come across this unusual edifice in Workman Gardens. Stretching up into the branches of a great spreading oak beside them, these jaw bones stand, lichen covered and looking almost as if they are part of a tree themselves.

They first belonged to an unfortunate whale captured off Hull in 1820 by the crew of the 'Andrew Marvel'. A member of the crew, a Mr Stanton who came from Evesham, presented the bones as a gift to his friend Dr Beale Cooper and for 80 years they stood in his garden in the Mansion house at the corner of Cooper's Lane and Waterside. Eventually, in 1906, Cooper's grand-daughter presented the jaw bones to the Borough, and so here they stand, firmly braced by metal bars and with more metal securing the apex. Their arrival at the good doctor's home must have created quite a stir, but now the people of Evesham appear to regard them with some amusement and affection, and when time and the weather finally takes its toll, their loss will be regretted.

HONEYBOURNE

From Russia with Love

Domestic Fowl Trust and Honeybourne Rare Breeds. 6 miles from Evesham, 1½ miles east of Bretforton, off B4035.
Map Reference: O.S. map 150 (1: 50,000); 115438

If Charlie doesn't look very happy, it is not because he's not well cared for. It's because he is so rare in Britain that as yet he doesn't have a mate. Charlie is a Spangled Russian Orloff cockerel, possibly the only one in the country, his breed found only in Iran and Russia. Just coming out of moult, some of his feathers already gleam bronze, turquoise and irridiscent greens again, and his legs boast spurs over two inches long. His neighbours here in Honeybourne include many breeds of hens, like the Crested Blue Poland (below), ducks, geese (American Buff, Toulouse and African) and Silver Pheasants, as well as rare breeds of cattle, pigs, Shetland ponies and sheep – including Grey-faced Dartmoors with coats which look as if they have been permed! Mr and Mrs Landshoff, who have taken over the preservation of rare breeds of farm animals, begun in 1979, hope to develop the Trust still further, and visitors are welcome throughout the year. The Trust is also always willing to help and advise poultry owners.

For further information ring 01386 833083.

42

BROADWAY
The Golden Wines of Autumn

Barnfield Winery and Cider Mill, nr Childswickham, 1½ miles north of Broadway off A44
Map Reference: O.S. map 150 (1: 50,000); 081383

Stone cider mills like this were used as far back as the 15th century, often outdoors and near the orchards. Still in working order this one, of Malvern stone, weighs about 8 tons in total (excluding the horse needed to work it!), the top weighing 3 tons and the base in 3 pieces because it is so heavy. Fruit is layered in the trough to become pulped as the horse pushes the wheel round. The pulp is then removed to a press. The press here, about 150 years old, of wood with steel re-inforcements, could produce up to 45 gallons of juice in each pressing, depending on the type of apple used. This drains into a gully and then into containers.

This winery was founded in 1925 by the Crump family and since 1986 has been in the hands of Mr Martin and his son, who have plans to refurbish the working area. Visitors are welcome to visit 7 days a week, to step back in time, see the old way of working and also to taste (free!) and buy, the variety of Wines, Cider and Perry made here. This, along with home produced jam, honey and eggs, could make for a very happy shopping experience!

LOWER WICK
St. Cuthbert's Barn

At Bennett's Dairy, Manor Farm, 1 mile west of Worcester on A449
Map Reference: O.S. map 138: (1: 50,000); 840527

Wick Barn, in the Dairy's farmyard, has had a long and varied career. Part of the east and west walls are thought to be the remains of St. Cuthbert's (St Johns mother church), built around 1165. St. Cuthbert, Bishop of Lindisfarne and later patron of shepherds and seafarers, died in 687. By 1371 the church was 'half deserted and attended by very few', but although the Bishop ordered it to be demolished, this did not happen. Instead, by the 1500s a large barn had been built on the church foundations – one of the beams has been carbon-dated to 1520 – and apart from some minor changes in the 17th and 18th centuries, the barn at Netherwick, as it was called, is as we see it today. It was used for storing fleeces in Worcester's heyday of wool production; soldiers probably sheltered there during the Powick battles of the Civil War; in the late 1600s it was used as a kind of workhouse, for records exist of 'poor'

and 'travelling' people dying there. In the first half of the 18th century when gaol fever broke out in Worcester's prison, prisoners were sent there – hence the bars on two windows. The next century saw it as successful hop barns and stables. Today, well maintained and cared for by its owner, Mr Bennett, it continues to guard its history, and still serves a useful life as part of the farm and Visitor's Centre.

POWICK
Water for All

Beside A449 to Malvern, 1 mile from Worcester beyond the Western Bypass roundabout
Map Reference: O.S. map 138: (1: 50,000); 835518.

Because this neat little building is beside a busy main road, many drive past without noticing it (and anyone wishing to find it is advised to park before looking!) But in pre-car days, the villagers of Powick came here regularly, grateful for its existence, for it was the village pump house. Built of red brick, it is still open to the world although no-one now needs to collect the well water it once provided. In earlier times some were happy to use water from the river, but this area is in a flood plain and once the dangers of contamination were realised, wells were dug and natural springs used. Then the pump house was built, so that for the last years of the 19th and into the beginning of the 20th centuries, villagers could shelter from the weather while using the old black hand pump above its shallow sink, to gather pure water for their needs.

KEMPSEY
'A Triplicity of Persons'

In St Mary's church, 5 miles south of Worcester down Church Lane off A 38.
Map Reference: O.S. map 150: (1: 50,000); 848490

This epitaph is included because of its unusual wording. Set high on the wall in St Andrew's Chapel in the south transept, it records the lives of the Rev. George Boulter, vicar here 1748-98, and of his two wives – '... *a Vicar, one Husband, Two Helpmeets, both Wives and both Anns, a Triplicity of Persons in two Twains but one Flesh ...*' The vicar's first wife, maiden name Hyde, died in 1757 when only 33. His second, Ann Hester, in 1774 aged 45, but the epitaph proudly refers to her being '*nearly allied by Consanguinity to Sir Joseph Jekyll Knt, Master of the Rolls*' (so the vicar married a Hyde and nearly a Jekyll!). Although his epitaph claims he was here for 30 years before he died aged 81, records show that the Rev Boulter was in fact vicar here for 50 years.

Another very personal memorial is that to Sir Edmund Wylde who lies to the left of the Altar, clad in armour, with sword sheath beneath him. High Sheriff of his County, he died in 1620 of a '*most painfull and greevous sikness*' and was '*solempnly here interred with great lamentation*' when only 32. One cannot help but wonder what caused so young a death.

SEVERN STOKE
A Stairway to Heaven

4 ½ miles south of Kempsey, turning off A 38 and down a lane to the church and the Rose and Crown.
Map Reference: O.S. map 150 (1: 50,000): 856440.

Climb up the stairs of the tower at the church of St Denys, and you will climb higher than the tower itself. The lower part of the tower in the position of a north transept, was built about 1300, while the upper parts were added about a century later. They are adorned with battlements, but for some reason, the builder forgot to stop building the steps and so the stair turret is higher than it should be. Sometimes the church is locked, but if you obtain a key, you will discover that the south aisle, arcade and font are 14th

century, while the rest of the interior is restored 19th and 20th century. It is said that here, during the Commonwealth period, one John Somers, whose family owned much of Severn Stoke, became angry with the minister as he preached in the pulpit, and shot at him. He missed, but it must have been a talking point for some time after!

UPTON ON SEVERN
Drink Outside

11 miles south of Worcester on A 4104, at Bridge End in the High Street.
Map Reference: O.S. Map 150 (1: 50,000); 852405

It is unusual to find now to find an hotel where 'non-Bar' drinkers are catered for, but the Star Hotel did just this. The window looks out on to narrow Dunns Lane and doubtless it once witnessed much business. In the late 19th century Upton had 4 inns and 11 taverns (as well as 6 bakers, 5 blacksmiths, 9 bootmakers and 9 maltsters among other trades). The Star was a coaching inn, advertised as a Posting House in 1838 and busy with coaches stopping twice a day on journeys between Malvern, Cheltenham and Worcester. It still has something of its old world atmosphere, with many original oak beams and fine panelled walls in the Oak Room. It is also reputed to have its own ghost, that of a lady who has an an affinity with Room 9. There she has been seen several times, it is said, standing by the window as if bent over a cradle. Ghost or not, the Star is an hotel with a past, now boasting the modern comforts of the present. It faces the 'Pepperpot', once a church and now a TIC which offers much information about Upton, an area conscious of its heritage and showing commendable civic pride in preserving and promoting it.

UPTON ON SEVERN
To lie in Parson's Field

About ½ mile beyond New St. off Cut Throat Lane and to the right of the Sewage Works.
Map Reference: O.S.map 150 (1: 50,000): 842406

Over a stile beside one of Upton's Walks and set in the corner of a peaceful field, lies this simple burial ground, a reminder of one of the horrors encountered by our forebears. Cholera visited Upton at the end of July in 1832. An unremarked death in over-crowded Lapstone Alley off Dunns Lane by the river, soon led to many more. People had little knowledge of basic hygiene, medicine was in its infancy, and within 2 weeks 18 had died. It was swift and severe. They stopped tolling the funeral bell – it became too frightening to listen to – and decided to bury cholera victims here in Parson's Field, ½ mile away from Upton itself. One of the victims was named Church, causing the wry comment that although these burials were away from the usual consecrated ground, there was at least a Church in Parson's Field. Within a month there had been 50 deaths, but other places suffered too. Between July and October in the same year in Worcester, there were 293 cases and 79 deaths. A stillness hangs over this ground now and one cannot help but utter a silent prayer of thanks for the benefits of modern knowledge and 21st century medicine.

RIPPLE
A Law-abiding Village

13 miles south of Worcester, 5 miles north west of Tewkesbury, off A 38.
Map Reference: O.S.map 150 (1: 50,000): 877378.

Ripple now, is a small but peaceful village and these stocks suggest that perhaps its inhabitants have always been encouraged, one way or another, to be law-abiding. An Act passed in 1405 decreed that every village should provide stocks and these, set now behind rails on the tiny village green, with a whipping post and in front of a 14th century Preaching Cross, have been well maintained. The green is surrounded by cottages, one pink-washed, with good old English names like Ripple, Ivy and Honeysuckle Cottage. The Cross was set at the junction of 2 old tracks between Worcester and Tewkesbury, Bredon and Midsummer Hill, Malvern, and in the old coaching

days travellers made a halt at Ripple Cottage, then an inn called The Nag's Head.

Nearby, the Norman church of St Mary, where work is currently being done, has much to interest the visitor, not least some beautiful misericords.

MALVERN
Pouring Blessings

½ mile from Great Malvern, toward Worcester, beside B4232, near the junction of A449
Map Reference: O.S. map 150 (1: 50,000); 773468.

This water tank with clock tower stands quietly on its own grassy patch near an entrance to the Worcester Way and the Tank Quarry picnic area. The tank was built in 1835/36 to provide water for this area by a local benefactor, Charles Morris Jun. The clock tower was added in 1901. At that time it was surrounded by the bustle and noise of quarrying, for from 1800, stone had been extracted here, mainly for building purposes. However, in 1970 this quarry, the last of the Pyx Quarries in North Malvern, closed down, approximately 13 million tons having been removed by then. Now Tank Quarry is peaceful and impressive. Nature has taken over the 100m high rock face – it extended a further 30m below the current level when it closed – and climbers should not be tempted, for it is known to be very dangerous. As for the tower, it bears a fading inscription, asking those upon whom Morris' abundance poured, to pray for an equal abundance of blessings to be poured upon him.

MALVERN
'Multum in Parvo'

In Great Malvern, down a narrow road opposite the Unicorn Inn, Belle Vue Terrace.
Map Reference: O.S. map 150 (1: 50,000); 775460.

'Much in Little' is the maxim of this theatre, officially the smallest theatre in the world (Guinness Book of Records June 2000). Measuring only 16ft in length and about 9ft wide, it is licensed to seat 12 people and is unique in being converted from a Convenience for Victorian gentlemen! Independent and non-profit making, it is the result of 3 years hard work using salvaged materials (in deference to its toilet origins, copper ballcocks grace the top of pillars!), work done on a shoe string by Dennis Neale and friends. But the result is striking – everything in miniature – bright red curtain, tiny stage, painted backcloth, facilities for

lighting and sound. 'Much in Little' applies to the ambitious programme too. Since its opening in November 1999, various events have been staged – plays, puppetry, children's workshops, poetry readings, storytelling, dance and music of all kinds, even a rock band concert! Anyone is welcome to use the theatre and during the summer the door is generally open to visitors. It is to be hoped that people will support it, for no theatre can succeed without an audience and players.

(For further information, telephone Dennis Neale on 01684 568933)

MALVERN PRIORY
Precious Tiles

Malvern Priory is the only building in the country which has such a remarkable and unique collection of Medieval mural tiles. Made between 1456 and about 1520, the tiles, more than 1200 in number and in 90 different patterns, are famous for both their designs and their standard of workmanship. They were all hand made in the monastery, sometimes using 4 tiles to make up a design. They have been painstakingly finished, most of the patterns glazed in colours of gold and brown. They were, for the most part, specially made to decorate the Choir screen although others were used on the floor. Now we may admire them where they have been carefully preserved on the wall in the apse, some faded but others in remakable condition.

But in lone splendour on one of the north pillars facing the entrance door, is an even more unusual tile. Again dated about 1456 and fired in a kiln at the east end of the church, it asks worshippers to be a 'friend' to the church by giving money now, rather than later in a bequest. Everyone would agree that it is a tile with a plea as relevant today as it was when it was fired nearly 550 years ago! The letters were printed on the tile by means of fixed type carved on to a wooden block. This was the same method by which the first books were printed before Gutenberg pioneered the use of movable type on paper in 1455.

LITTLE MALVERN PRIORY
For Dissolute Monks?

4 miles south of Great Malvern on A4104 to Welland.
Map Reference: O.S. map 150 (1: 50,000); 770404

Parts of this Benedictine Priory date back to 1171 when Brothers Edred and Joceline broke away from Worcester to found this cell of their own. They dedicated it to St Giles, but Monks here do not appear to have been very hard-working or devout – which is perhaps why they sought independence in the first place. Within 9 years, 'by reason of their demerits' and because of 'the great ruin of the church and place', Bishop Alcock sent them to Gloucester for re-instruction, while the Priory was rebuilt and a new Prior installed. It was still a working cell in 1538 when it was dissolved, although by then it only had 1 Prior and 6 Monks. Only the chancel, tower and transept of the church remain, but it may be visited at certain times, as occasionally may the Court by its side. This was originally a Medieval house which formed part of the monastic buildings, and now, much restored, is a private house.

The legend of Ragged Stone Hill which rises behind the Priory, is linked with a Monk here. He fell in love, and as a punishment for breaking his vows, had to crawl each day to the top of the hill. One day he cursed the hill and everyone who fell in its shadow – a story some remember, as clouds cast shadows over this area.

GADFIELD ELM

For the Brethren

On Gloucestershire border, 8 miles from Welland, 1 mile south of Pendock, off B4208.
Map Reference: O.S. map 150 (1: 50,000); 786314

It is easy to pass this small building since it has its back to the country road on which it stands, and yet it is a place of great significance to members of the Church of the Latter Day Saints. Restored and re-dedicated in the summer of 2000, it was here in 1836 that U.K. Brethren, of whom there were about 600, built Gadfield Elm Chapel, the world's first Chapel of Latter Day Saints. Evangelists John Benbow* and Wilford Woodruff preached here and it was the religion's focal point until 1842, when it was sold to help the thousands of brethren who migrated to America. At that time, within a radius of 15 miles, there were 40 congregations. This then, is the only surviving memorial to the United Brethren who joined and then became missionaries for the Church of the Latter Day Saints. The building is austere, with plain stone walls, and a double row of pine benches forming pews which seat about 100. There is no altar, but a lectern before an open fire.

A key is obtainable nearby and there are picnic tables and a small car park set off the road.

* See Benbow Pool at Castle Frome, Herefordshire (ref Curiosities of Herefordshire, Ann Moore, p.22).

MARTLEY
Sleep Safely

7 miles north of Worcester, off B4204.
Map Reference: O.S. map 150 (1: 50,000): 756598

Here is a reminder of a time when graves were plundered for any surgeon who would pay for a corpse to further medical science. This small grave, securely banded by iron hoops, bears neither name nor date, although just before I visited someone had placed there a small jar of flowers. Its size suggests it is that of an infant, and the bands perhaps underline the grief felt by parents who wished to ensure the sanctity of the grave, possibly before 1832 when an Act of Parliament made body-snatching illegal. The grave lies to the left of the path on the turn beneath blossom trees which meet in an arch, and is in stark contrast to those in the main well-kept church yard. There some parents have recorded their grief at losing their 'little princess' by leaving toys and teddy bear wreaths to watch over their child.

Inside this red sandstone church of St Peter, the medieval wall paintings (recorded in the earlier Worcestershire Curiosities), are well worth seeing.

Although there is a parking area by the church gate, some may prefer to park beside the B4204 where spaces are provided, for the lane opposite which leads down to the church is narrow.

MARTLEY
Do Drop In!

About ½ mile further along B4204, at the junction with the B4197.
Map Reference: O.S. map 150 (1: 50,000); 743600

This small neat building, now more than a century old, is a good example of the 'change of usage' rule. Set on a little Green of its own, this was built in 1895 as part of a public weighbridge, very useful for members of Martley Parish who wished to weigh large quantities of farm produce, bricks or stone. (See also Ombersley p.65). Now the pit has been filled in, but the building, housing a table and two chairs, still serves a useful function in the community. Besides being a centre for parish notices, it is also used as a Police 'drop in' centre every Tuesday morning. A notice advises those wishing to contact the law, that on that day they should 'Look for the car'!

KYRE
A Grand Dove House

7 miles from Bromyard, 4 miles south west of Tenbury on B4214. Follow the signs to Kyre Church.
Map Reference: O.S. Map 138 (1: 50,000); 626636

This handsome Norman dovecote was once an essential feature of life in England, providing welcome fresh meat for the lord of the manor. Part of Kyre Park for centuries, it was moved to its present position behind the 16th century tithe barn (now living a busy life as Toy City) in the 1750s. It was at about that time that the Georgian features were added to the house as well as to the dove-cote – the dormer windows and the arched doorway. The original door, just over 4 feet high, is at the back of

the dove-cote. Inside, it still retains its ladder by which one reached the pigeons or squabs (baby birds) in their nesting holes which are set in double rows round the walls, numbering well over 1000.

KYRE
Rapunzel's Tower

It is refreshing to be able to feature a modern 'folly' in a book mainly concerned with 'curiosities' from the past, but here in Kyre Gardens Rapunzel's Tower deserves such inclusion. It was built only a few years ago as part of the restoration of the gardens undertaken by the new owners since 1994, and was designed 'with our daughter in mind'.

At that time she had long hair – though she hasn't now! – and it really is a fairy tale castle, with its own waterfalls, and streams, River God's cave and grotto and a tiny bridge nearby. Still to be completed, it must enchant any child (and adult!) and adds charm to gardens which are in themselves so enjoyable to wander through.

Kyre Park is open daily from February to the end of December, and although the house may not be visited, the delightful gardens and nursery, the tearooms and Toy City shop make a pleasant afternoon out for any visitor. Enquiries on 01885 410247.

GRIMLEY
A Victorian Stairway

1½ miles northwest of Worcester, turning off A443 beyond Hallow.
Map Reference: O. S. map 150 (1: 50,000); 836607

There is no mistaking the entrance to the Church of St Bartholomew, for the original Norman door is framed by a Norman style porch set beside an arcaded stairway leading up to the west gallery. The effect is striking – a church with a sense of its own importance, as indeed it should have, since it is over 800 years old and was once, before the Reformation, part of the Manor held by the Worcester Priors.

It was in 1845 that the Victorians, replacing a timber structure with a new tower, built the porch and the stairway, the steps of which are already beginning to show hollows worn by the feet of those using them.

HOLT
Smile Please!

2 miles from Hallow going along A443 towards Great Witley, turning off down a narrow
road on the right (signposted)
Map Reference: O.S.map 150 (1:50,000); 829626

This grinning face greets anyone who visits the red sandstone Church of St
Martin. The carvings are of Norman origin, as is the building, and looking
at them, you are forced to smile back, even though a padlock prevents you
entering their church. The register here goes back to 1538, and in February
1655 a marriage was celebrated between one Richard Danes and Joanne
Pritchett, the banns being published in the market place at Worcester
between *'the howers of eleven and two'*!

Leaving the church, one cannot help but stand and gaze at Holt Castle
opposite.

HOLT
An Englishman's Home …

Holt Castle's imposing tower, built in the 14th century by Sir John Beauchamp, stands firm, while much of the medieval castle around it has been rebuilt and extended. Holt manor was first granted to the D'Abitot family by William the Conqueror. Sir John was the last of the Beauchamps here, and later the Castle became home to Sir Henry Bromley, recorded in history as having tracked four of the Gunpowder Plotters to Hindlip Hall, a Catholic stronghold, since demolished and now the site of Police Headquarters near the Worcester City boundary. Sir Henry was courteous to the Catholic 'traitors' Oldcorne and Garnett, entertaining them here at his home before taking them to London to stand trial for their faith. Still a private home, Holt Castle is not open to visitors unless they are using the Conference Rooms set aside for that purpose.

OMBERSLEY
The House that Moved

8 miles north of Worcester off A449, opposite car park of The Crown and Sandys.
Map Reference: O.S.map 150 (1: 50,000); 845634

These two private cottages were once one house and the date on the gable tells us when the change took place. Originally 16th or early 17th century, this building began life in Bewdley as a centre for the Pewterer's Guild (there is still a lane called Pewterer's Alley in Wribbenhall over the bridge from Bewdley). Then in 1841, in a state of disrepair, it was bought by the 2nd Baron Sandys of Ombersley, Lord Arthur Moyses Hill, and re-erected here. Each porch has different ballusters – deliberate, or the fault of the carpenter, one onders.

At the south end the Baronet's coronet stands over 2 Ss entwined – S for Sandys and for Stirling, a 17th century ancestor of the family. The griffin rampant on the north side is one of the supporters of the family coat of arms. Ombersley was first leased from the crown as a manorial estate by the Sandys family in 1587, and it is thanks to their care and vigilance that the village has retained its character and its charm.

OMBERSLEY
A Splendid old 'Tree' House

Just beyond the roundabout, on the corner of Holt Fleet Road, stands this splendid example of a cruck house. Built before 1500, it shows quite clearly the principle behind this type of building, so common at that time. Each gable end was fashioned from natural curved timber, generally oak, which formed an arch, with each foot set on stone to prevent rotting and then in-filled with wattle and daub. Originally the house would have consisted of a 2 bay hall, an upper room (solar), and servants' quarters, the whole being thatched. 'Cresswells', as it is called, was, during the last century, a sweet shop and newsagent's, run by a lady whose husband was the village builder, carpenter and coffinmaker. A grade II listed building, it has been well maintained and sympathetically restored to become a 4 bedroomed home, keeping many of its original ceiling beams, with some exposed brickwork and now worth something over £250,000.

What changes this building must have seen over the centuries!

OMBERSLEY
A Weighing Station

Facing Cresswells across the busy roundabout, is another, much 'younger' building, but still one with its own history – a history which, like the Pewterer's House, involved moving. The hut, part of a weighbridge, began life as a result of an Act which demanded that Rural District Councils should provide Weighing machines for public use. (see also Martley, p. 57).

But it did not stand here until the roundabout was built in 1935, when it was moved in sections from its original position south of Cresswells across the road. It recorded the weight of vehicles and their loads, and it was used by local farmers until it became defunct in 1977. Since that date, the hut has been used for storing the parish council's garden equipment and is now empty, but occasionally opened as a small local heritage centre displaying pictures relating to Ombersley's past. The trough to its left beneath the trees on the Green was a plague stone where, in the 14th century, food was left for sufferers by well-wishers.

ASTLEY
Weathered but Worthy

2½ miles south west of Stourport off A451 from Great Witley.
Map Reference: O.S. map 150 (1:50,000); 788678

Here is a door which appears to be weathering the test of time quite successfully. Solid, metal studded and with fine hinges, it has seen many attempts to preserve its life – at some time it even appears to have been hung upside down! St Peter's church stands in a commanding position on a rise, and dates back to 1102 when Ralph de Tondini founded a Priory here, although the Prior's Well at the east end of the church is all that remains of that. The nave, chancel and doorway are Norman, as is the relief of a small head on one of the pillars on the north side of the nave arcade. He must have gazed down on worshippers over the centuries, the image of a mischievous stone-mason, perhaps, who wished to be remembered for ever. Like the rest of St Peter's he has been well cared for.

The church grounds are the resting place of Frances Ridley Havergal, writer of hymns, born at the Rectory here in 1836, and buried in June 1879 at the side of the churchyard, beneath a tree near the lane.

ARELEY KINGS
A Retreat from Domestic Cares

1 mile south of Stourport off A451 from Great Witley.
Map Reference: O.S. map 138 (1: 50,000): 802712

What do we all like to do when things get too much for us? Escape, escape from 'domestic worries' – and this is just what a Rector of St Bartholomew's did in Areley Kings. In 1728 the Rev. Richard Vernon had this outstout built in the church grounds, specifically for his use only. His 'outside study' as he called it, contained bookshelves, a stout door to keep the world at bay and fine views over the fields and the River Severn. When the church was rebuilt in 1885 (rebuilt apart from its 12th century chancel and 14th century tower), the Victorian Rector probably thought it was a good idea to refurbish this building too, for it looks in remarkable condition. Perhaps he, like his predecessors, maybe surrounded by a household of women and weighed down by parochial cares, welcomed the escape his 'den' could provide. He would not be the only man to do so! In more recent years the building has been used for storage, occasional Guide or Scout meetings – and even, it is whispered, as a place of assignation!

ROCK
So Give Alms …

5 miles south east of Bewdley off A456 to Leominster.
Map Reference: O.S. map 138 (1: 50,000); 732711.

Through the ages men have been taxed – after all, the Domesday Book was a tax census- and for the people of Rock it was no different. The oldest piece of 'furniture' in the Church of St Peter and St Paul is this alms chest. Henry II (1154-1189) decreed that in every parish there should be a chest for collecting money for the Crusades, and when Pope Innocent became Pope in 1198 he added that such chests should be made of a hollowed out tree trunk and fastened with three locks. Thus three key-holders must attend its opening. Over the centuries, especially after an Act of 1552, vicars, as part of religious instruction, 'gently exhorted' their parishioners to give for relief of the poor – and now we fill out our tax returns! This chest is clearly very old, although modifications have been made over the years. Metal studded, it measures 72 ins by 15 ins, with a depth of 13 ins. The centre opens to reveal the money box, 31 ins long and 8 ins wide. It is a large and rare artifact. Indeed there is much of interest here, a church said to be the largest Norman village church in the county. The carvings above the chancel arch are particularly impressive.

ROCK
A Sharp Punishment

This whipping post was made at a time when the poorer members of society found life very difficult. People often had large families, poverty was rife in spite of the Poor Law and in areas such as this, relying on agriculture and the Forest, work was hard to find, squatters arrived in the Forest and social unrest grew. The whipping post, which stands just over 4 ½ feet high, was erected in 1773, the metal cuffs designed to secure miscreants of any height. John Wainwright, a carpenter later put in charge of the parish workhouse, made the accompanying stocks (for three!) in 1782. Together they stood outside the church, but such punishments were not new. There is a record of the same deterrants in Worcester's Corn Market in 1694, when the 'whip man' could be paid as much as 4d for each public whipping. How would modern vandals view such public humiliations now, one wonders.

The Rock stocks were used for the last time in 1860 and are now preserved, with the post, inside the church.

(See also Ripple)

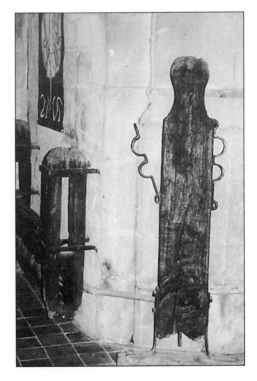

ROCK
No More Wind and Rain

It's not easy to discover just how long this weathercock stood proudly on top of the Church of St Peter and St Paul, but his design and the workmanship suggest that he is old. We do know that he was re-gilded in 1935 by church warden Walter Seager when a flagpole was renewed, and that he was finally brought indoors later, in 1966, when the pole was removed (it was renewed again in 1978). In 1966, when the organ was moved to its present position, our cockerel was fixed securely to a stool. Now, instead of swinging gently in the wind and rain, he surveys the congregation from his high, (and dry) perch beside the organ. From there he has an excellent 'bird's eye view' of the highly decorated chancel arch already mentioned – the intricate Norman carvings of other birds and centaurs, of allegories and quatrefoils – all work justly more famous than a gilded weathercock once regarded as an important part of local weather lore.

STOURPORT
Up the Winding Staircase

12 miles from Worcester via A451 or B4194, beside the riverside car park.
Map Reference: O.S.map 138 (1: 50,000); 808711

Stourport Bridge over the River Severn was completed in 1870 and this unusual spiral staircase will lead you up to the main road from the riverside. The first bridge, built of local stone and replacing a ferry and ford, was erected in 1775 shortly after Brindley created this artificial inland port as part of the Staffordshire and Worcestershire Canal system. Stourport, as it became known, is one of the few towns in England to come into being as the result of canal engineering. Today's bridge was a toll bridge until tolls ceased in April 1893, but one cannot help but wonder why it was felt necessary to design these steps as spiral, difficult for late Victorian and Edwardian ladies to negotiate, – or was this a 'gentlemen only' staircase?

STOURPORT
A Cupola Clock

Via Engine Lane opposite the Bridge Inn from the main riverside carpark. 138; 810711

The building beneath the unusual clock tower is one of the original canal buildings, once a warehouse and now home to the local Motor Yacht Club. The clock and tower, almost unique now, were erected in 1813 by public subscription. 71 people gave between one and ten guineas to reach a total of £247. 16s. The clock was made by Samuel Thorpe (1790 – 1836) a great clock maker from Abberley who made all manner of sundials, watches and clocks, including those at Great Witley Church, Rock, Glasshampton and Brockhampton. This one, with mechanical features unique to Thorpe's work, had ¼ chimes, gilded cast iron numerals on each of its four dials and four pinnacles on the cupola which survived into the 1920s. When the turret was repaired in 1993, white numerals replaced the originals. Since the Clock Warehouse is such an historical feature of the Canal Basins, it is to be hoped that this valuable example of Thorpe's work will continue to tell us the time well into the 21st century and beyond.

STOURPORT
Share and Share Alike

Continue along Engine Lane towards Mart Lane.

The Tontine Hotel looks out over the river and the Canal Basins, a fine Georgian building included here because of the unusual financial implications of its name. A tontine, originally the idea of one Lorenzo Tonti in the 1650s, refers to a group of people who participate financially in a project, thereby securing a kind of life annuity which increases as the subscribers die until the last survivor inherits all. The hotel was built by the Canal Company in 1773, soon after the canal opened. It had a ballroom and commercial rooms, the wings being used as offices and dwellings for merchants whose trade was mainly based on grain, hops and farm products. It was often the centre for regattas and parties too, and today it is still a handsome building, a proud reminder of the days when Stourport's Canal Basin was a busy centre for waterborne trade.

RIBBESFORD
Is it a Fish?

North west of Stourport,1 mile south west of Bewdley down an avenue off B4194.
Map Reference; O.S. map 138 (1: 50,000); 787740

Is it a fish, a beaver or a duck-billed platypus? This unusual carving over the door into St Leonard's Church dates back to 1100. At one time the villeins of the manor of 'Ribeford' were bound to *'furnish wears (weirs) and nets for catching fish and proper implements for hunting'* and here we see depicted an archer who was so skilful that with one arrow he killed both a deer and a – salmon? Or has he killed a monster pursuing the deer? The old legend was celebrated by a Mr Griffiths whose verse ends as below* Fortunately the porch, built in 1633 and commemorating the unknown TM and HW by their initials, has protected the carving on the tympanum so that you may decide for yourself

> ** Just as he pulled his well-tried bow*
> *And as his arrow flew*
> *Upleaped a salmon – thus the doe*
> *And salmon both he slew.*

RIBBESFORD
Play Piggy, Play

It is a surprise to come upon St Leonard's, tucked away down a tree lined avenue, but there is much of interest here – a timbered bell cote, with one of its three bells possibly 13th century, and if so the oldest in Worcestershire, and more carvings. These are now on the pulpit, though formerly they were part of a 15th century rood screen; a pig playing the bagpipes and a fox preaching to geese. The fox, clad in a cloak, is said to represent one of the many begging Friars who were so disliked by local Priests.

St Leonard, who died about 559 AD and patron saint of prisoners, lived at one time as a hermit, but later went on to found a monastery at Noblac in France.

To the side of the church, among trees, lies the handsome turreted Ribbesford House, built in 1820 on the site of a fortified manor complete with moat and drawbridge (now gone). It is a private house and cannot be visited, but it is a reminder that until the 16th century Ribbesford used to be more important than Bewdley.

BLACKSTONE
Get away from it all

As seen from the Country Park, continuing from Ribbesford on B4194, or off B4195.
Map Reference: O.S. map 138 (1: 50,000); 793741

The red sandstone rock which dominates the River Severn on the eastern side – and is somewhat surprisingly called 'Black' stone – is not easy to approach now that modern highways surround it. It is an imposing sight, looking strong as a fortress, entrances in its face leading to what Nash, writing in the 1700s, called *'a curious subterraneous vault divided into a cell for the habitation of a hermit, and a chapel for his religious worship'*. The hermitage was in fact lived in at various times during the 12th and 13th centuries, and one legend relates to one of its tenants. Sir Harry Wade looked forward to his wedding to his fair bride, Alice Clopton of Stratford, but un-beknown to Sir Harry, he had a rival. Just as they were about to wed, Alice was snatched away. Harry gave chase, but in the fight than ensued, Alice fell from a bridge and was drowned. Her abductor escaped, but Harry, heartbroken, retired here to Blackstone where, in his sorrow, he lived the life of a recluse. Ten years later, he was still living here, when one day Alice's abductor came to beg forgiveness. That was too much for Sir Harry. In a rage, he took the man and flung him from the cliff face, killing him. Some versions of the story say he drowned, but whatever the man's end, Sir Harry was surely avenged for the loss of his bride.

Nash tells us, too, that in the 1700s the hermitage was *'profanely turned into a cyder mill and cellar'* something he obviously disapproved of. Perhaps he would have approved of the use it was put to during the Second World War. In 1940, after the Southampton factory which made Spitfires was bombed, Lord Beaverbrook dispersed component production to various small workshops, with the finished work being assembled at Castle Bromwich, and ordered that all production tools should be duplicated and stored away. Steatite and Porcelain Products Ltd made vital components for aircraft radar sets, and a plaque in the hermitage records that at that time their dies and press tools were stored here. Blackstone is not just a rock, but a rock with a long history.

BEWDLEY
A Centre of History

3 miles north of Stourport on B4194
Map Reference: O.S. map 138 (1: 50,000); 788751

This handsome neo-classical building in Load Street, with its mermaid and merman sculpture, reflects the importance Bewdley attaches to the Guildhall, its civic centre. Built in 1808, it sits happily next to the Old Post Office (once a 17th century farm house) and across from a genuine Georgian coaching inn of 1765, and fronts 18th century Shambles, now a museum. Bewdley, or Beau Lieu, is truly an historic town, full of unique charm and once an important centre of trade from the River Severn. Waterborne traffic had begun early, in the 12th century at least, first on wooden rafts, later by trows. And the bow hauliers who worked these boats were strong and powerful, protective of their trade until it finally faded away leaving other local industries to continue.

No doubt the hauliers often ended hard-working days in an inn and then, perhaps, in prison overnight to cool off. The old bridge had a prison in the gatehouse, but enter the Guildhall's grand, wide entrance, and a short walk will bring you to this heavily studded, thrice bolted door. It is one of three cells, thought to date from 1802, which replaced the one on the bridge, Small, bleak and practically windowless, with only a tiny grate and a stone bench for a bed, they make an effective deterrant to a life of crime. They are at the end of the Shambles, built in 1783 to replace a late 15th century one, and now a museum. Here were 32 butchers' stalls in 2 arcades either side of the walkway. The arcades again reflect Bewdley's past, with displays of old local crafts. These include charcoal burning, coopering, an old brass foundary, the making of clay pipes and ropes, and a basket making workshop presented, fittingly enough, by a Mr Birch who was the last besom and basket maker in Bewdley.

WRIBBENHALL
Here's a Health …

Found by leaving Bewdley via Telford's bridge on to the B4190
Map Reference: O.S. map 138 (1: 50,000); 790754

Cross Telford's bridge out of Bewdley and you will find on your right the Black Boy Inn, unusual because, as you see, the figure on the sign is not that of a 'black boy' but of Charles II. During the Civil War Bewdley and this hostelry, were staunchly Royalist. After the Battle of Worcester, the King returned to exile, but in his absence his supporters could not show their loyalty to him for fear of persecution. But Charles II is said to have had a swarthy complexion, and so his followers found a way of registering their support of him without fear of reprisal. Raising their glasses, they would drink to the health of 'The Black Boy across the Water', so signalling their loyalty as they awaited the King's return.

This area of Bewdley is known as Catchems End, a name which dates back to 1472 and the Wars of the Roses when Bewdley was granted a Charter of Incorporation. This, in effect, made it a town of sanctuary. Thus, fugitives from justice wishing to enter Bewdley for sanctuary, waited here until they could cross the river to safety under cover of darkness – unless of course, one of the guards managed to 'catch em' first!

KINLET
A Place to Reminisce

5½ miles north west of Bewdley along B4194 at the crossroads with B555
Map Reference: O.S. map 138 (1: 50,000): 718803

Where would you find a 1920s petrol pump facing you in a pub bar in the 21st century? Answer: in the Eagle and Serpent at Kinlet. Strictly speaking, the Eagle is in the County of Shropshire, but its postal address in Bewdley, Worcestershire and it has a Dudley post code so, for these reasons alone, it must qualify for inclusion in a 'curiosities' book! But the place itself is full of curiosities too – lamps, posters, farming implements, old radios – so many objects collected over the last 30 years by owner and proprietor Gil Tibbutts. He took over the 320 year old building 2 years ago after it had been closed for 2 years and is currently bringing it back to life. Most of the items date from the 1940s and 50s, and very soon Gil hopes to convert the garage into an area where he can display his memorabilia beside vintage motor cycles and cars (including a red vehicle reminiscent of

Jones' 'Dad's Army' van). The pub is open 7 days a week, lunchtimes and evenings, and serves meals as well as drink. Anyone who likes reminiscing would enjoy taking a drive out to the Eagle and Serpent to experience these curiosities for himself.

WYRE FOREST
A Curly-Whirly Tree

3 miles west of Bewdley on A4117
Map Reference: O.S. map 138 (1: 50,000); 750743

Many children living near the Wyre Forest will be familiar with the Curly Whirly tree, one of nature's own curiosities. It is thought that when the tree was a sapling, a heavy snowfall pushed the slender stem down under a stronger branch nearby. Thereafter, being unable to spring back straight, the sapling had to grow up and out toward the light, forming the unusual shape we now see. Curly Whirly is not too far from the Visitors' Centre, along the shortest of four well marked woodland trails, suitable for people of all abilities. Managed by the Forestry Commission, the Wyre Forest is one of the largest areas of semi-natural woodland in the country and it is well worth a visit. There you may enjoy peaceful walks among birds and butterflies and look for great ants' nests and fallow deer, as you follow one of the tracks to find another notable tree – the unique and rare Whitty Pear. The trails in this working forest are open daily as are the picnic facilities, restaurant and the informative Visitors' Centre (though the latter are closed on Christmas Day).

UPPER ARLEY
A 'Folly' Tower

5 miles north west of Kidderminster, turning off A442 to Bridgenorth at Bellman's Cross; or by walking from Severn Valley's Arley Station and across the footbridge.
Map Reference O.S. Map 138 (1: 50,000); 765804.

This is a tower which was built, it is said, to spite a neighbour. It was the work of Lord Valentia, later Earl Mountnorris, lord of the manor here, who, in the late 1700s refurbished the church, built a school and extended the vicarage which stands to the right of the tower. He also remodelled Arley Hall, now gone, as a castle. It is said that the landlord of a local inn, Sam Willcox, would not sell the Earl a house which he wanted and so, to block Willcox's view, he built the tower – thereby also keeping from his own view The Valentia (now Hafren House). Mountnorris died in 1844. The tower, valued at £90,000 in 1987, has been refurbished and is now a private house.

Walking from here up Frenchman's Street to St Peter's Church is a stiff climb, but there you will find the tomb of a Crusader, thought to be Walter de Bohun. He was killed on his wedding day in a tournament while in Southampton, waiting to leave for the Holy Land.

At one time this area could be reached by a ferry operated by a rope and chain, a ferry which had been in operation since the 1300s at least. The footbridge took its place in 1972.

WOLVERLEY
Stay!

3 miles north of Kidderminster at the junction of B4190 from Bewdley and B4189 to Stourbridge.
Map Reference: O.S. map 138 (1:50,000); 828792

At the foot of the hill on which stands the church of St John the Baptist lies this rare animal pound. Carved out of natural sandstone, the thick walls and gate enclose the space, complete with three arched alcoves, where stray animals were impounded 'until ransomed by their owners'. These pounds, in some areas called 'pinfolds', were in use as early as the 16th century when parishes were required to provide them. Owners had to pay to retrieve their animals – in the Isle of Man it was at one time, a penny a hoof! It is doubtful if strays in Wolverly now would live long enough to be impounded, for this is situated at a crossroads and the gate fronts on to the busy B4189.

BLAKESHALL
A 'Safe' House

On a minor road, north of Wolverley, ½ mile south of Kingsford Country Park
Map Reference: O.S. map 138 (1: 50,000); 831812

At a time in the 16th and early 17th centuries when Catholics were hunted down and persecuted for their belief, finding a 'safe house' was a tricky business. How could you know whether the householder was sympathetic to recusants? How could you be sure that he would not give you away to intolerant officers of the law? If you knew where to look, the barn walls at Seabright Farm sent out a coded message. Each of the walls is studded with rows of small square ventilation holes, but look carefully at the wall facing the fields and away from the farm itself. There you will see five larger holes set in a straight row above the doorways and about six feet from the ground. They were known as 'the five wounds of Christ' and any Catholic visiting this farm could be sure of help and a safe lodging before he continued his journey. Even overgrown as the barn is here, the message is still there, a unique feature, and it must have been a welcome sight for any Catholic fearing for his life.

KIDDERMINSTER
A Fragment of the Past

¼ mile south from the Town Hall, in Castle Road between the Fire Station and the canal.
Map Reference: O.S. map 138 (1: 50,000); 831763

Like many towns, much of Kidderminster's past has been swept away. Caldwell Tower is one of its few remaining historically significant buildings, once part of the much larger, late 14th century Caldwell Castle. The rest of the Castle was demolished in 1700 and was replaced by a brick building which finally collapsed in 1961. Shortly after that, excavation workers found some Norman pottery and the boss from a Saxon shield, as well as an early 14th century penny. At that time the estate was owned by the Cokesay family (1347-1498). The tower is 3 storeys high, the ground floor much as it was, but on the north side lower than the road now, so that modern cars rush by just a little below the level of the first floor. Restored in the 1970s, the Tower shows that originally it must have been part of a very fine building. no wonder that it looks a little lost now.

Curiosities are everywhere!

BIBLIOGRAPHY

Brassington W.S.   *Historic Worcestershire.*
Gwilliam Bill   *Worcestershire's Hidden Past*
Havins P.J.N.   *Portrait of Worcestershire*
Hurle P.   *Upton*
Lloyd D.   *A History of Worcestershire*
Marsh J.   *Bewdley, a 15th Century Town*
Nash T.   *A History of Worcestershire*
Noake J   *Notes and Queries for Worcestershire*
Richards A. and S.   *Bromsgrove Now and Then*
Roelofsz E.   *A Millennium History of Ombersley and Doverdale*
Thompson R.D.   *Rock*
Wilkes N.   *A History of Eckington*

The Victoria County History.

The Kempsey Collection – published by St Mary's Church, Kempsey

The Journal of Prior William Moore – transcript published by Worcester History Society

Worcestershire Countryside Treasures – Worcestershire County Council

ACKNOWLEDGEMENTS

No-one can prepare a book like this without help and information from many people. Apart from those mentioned in the text, I must also thank some, briefly met, who were strangers – like Graham Taylor in Feckenham – as well as others whose name I never knew. Thanks, too, to Mr Somerton, Mr Bennett, Mr Glazzard, Mr Stan Jones and Dave, Mrs Landshoff, Mr Dudley Matthews MBE, and in particular to Shiela Hodges, Pauline and Terry Beale and Mr Jack Cluly who were most gererous in their help. I am also indebted to Tim Bridges of the Worcester City Museum Service, whose interest and knowledge spurred me on, to the staff of the Worcester Archeological Service and the County Record Office, to the ladies in the Tourist Information Centres at Bewdley and Evesham, to Mr David Chatham for photographing the Pershore sculpture and even to someone in the offices at South Staffordshire Water PLC in Walsall! I feel I have made many new friends. Finally, my especial thanks to Jon of Eyelevel Books whose patience and expertise brought it all together – and to my family for allowing me the time and space to research and explore in the first place!

INDEX